contemporary outlines from isaiah

paul tassell

BAKER BOOK HOUSE
Grand Rapids, Michigan

PHOTOLITHOPRINTED BY CUSHING - MALLOY, INC.
ANN ARBOR, MICHIGAN, UNITED STATES OF AMERICA
1979

AUTHOR'S PREFACE

This book contains outlines for each of the chapters of the book of Isaiah. The author prepared these outlines as he preached through these books in his pastoral ministry. More preaching ought to be done from these Old Testament books since conditions abound in our land today which were prevalent in the days of Isaiah. Many of the tremendous problems which face us today religiously, politically, and morally are diagnosed by these prophets. After diagnosing the problems, Isaiah courageously and clearly prescribes the proper and necessary treatment.

The message of this prophet is amazingly relevant to our needs today. It is with this in mind that the author desires to place before his readers in concise but pungent form these timeless truths.

Isaiah spoke to the men of his day, but also prophesied future events as he spoke and wrote under the inspiration of the Holy Spirit. These prophetic truths should be studied carefully and prayerfully realizing that the same God who fulfilled the prophecies concerning the first coming of Jesus Christ literally will also fulfill the prophecies concerning His second coming literally. Jesus Christ will come as a King, Israel will ultimately possess Palestine, the Millennial reign will be a literal, earthly reign, and the judgment of God upon wicked nations will certainly fall. These truths need to be emphasized in our day.

Paul Tassell

INTRODUCTION TO ISAIAH

Very little biographical material is available on Isaiah. The prophet gives us glimpses into his life and work in his writings, but we find few details to satisfy our curiosity. His name means "Salvation of Jehovah." Isaiah 7:3 and 8:3 tell us that the prophet was married and the father of two sons. The names of the sons are significant: Shear-Jashub means "a remnant shall return"; Maher-Shalal-Hash-Baz means "Haste ye, haste ye to the spoil."

The ministry of Isaiah the Prophet was a difficult one. His message was given in a time of great crisis, both politically and religiously. Isaiah prophesied from about 740 B.C. until about 680 B.C. This means that Isaiah had a long ministry extending from the final years of Uzziah through the reigns of Jotham, Ahaz and Hezekiah.

Isaiah's prophecy is divided into two definite sections. Chapters 1-39 deal primarily with the message of judgment and warning. Chapters 40-66 may be summarized in the words of the first two verses of Chapter 40, "Comfort ye, comfort ye my people, saith your God. Speak ye comfortably to Jerusalem." Chapters 1-39 deal with retribution; chapters 40-66 with restoration. This general division is quite apparent to the student as he reads and studies the prophet.

Isaiah was evidently a very courageous man. He had access to the highest authorities of his day. He was well-educated and possessed tremendous abilities as an author and public speaker. Isaiah was doubtless a man of great conviction, yet he had along with that conviction a great concern for the welfare of his people. He endeavored to be faithful to God while at the same time being completely honest with his people. This was no easy task for a man to perform in a day when so many of his contemporaries were compromising, time-serving pawns of idolatrous leaders.

CONTENTS

1. DEITY'S DREADFUL DIAGNOSIS OF MAN
Isaiah 1:5, 6

The prophets were never guilty of minimizing man's sins. They spoke under the inspiration of the Spirit of God, and their listeners were never spared the truth. Isaiah's diagnosis of Israel's condition reminds us of what Paul said about man's condition in Romans 3:10-18. Neither description flatters humanity. Both Isaiah and Paul knew that only as men were convinced and convicted of their sin would they see their desperate need of a Saviour. Isaiah's diagnosis centered on three major areas of man's makeup.

I. The Whole HEAD Is SICK. Isaiah 1:5

    A. *Reprobate* in their thinking. Isaiah shows the results of man's reprobate mind in Isaiah 1:21-23. In Romans 1:28, the Apostle Paul reveals that this sinful, reprobate mind is unregenerate man's portion because "they did not like to retain God in their knowledge."

    B. *Rebellious* in their attitude. Again, the Apostle Paul reminds us that "the carnal mind is enmity against God: for it is not subject to the law of God . . ." (Romans 8:7).

II. The Whole HEART Is FAINT. Isaiah 1:5

    A. Man is afflicted with a desperately wicked heart. Jeremiah 17:9

    B. This results in religious hypocrisy. Isaiah 1:11-15

    C. The Lord Jesus Christ quoted Isaiah when He said: "This people draweth nigh unto me with their mouth, and honoreth me with their lips; but their heart is far from me" (Matthew 15:8). What was true of sinful men in Isaiah's day was true in Christ's day, and it is still true today.

III. The Whole BODY Is CORRUPT. Isaiah 1:6

    A. Sowing to the flesh always reaps corruption. Galatians 6:8a

    B. The foolishness of sin always leaves the stench of its corruption. Psalm 38:5

What is the cure for man's malady? Isaiah also has that. "Come now, and let us reason together, saith the Lord: though your sins be as scarlet, they shall be as white as snow; though they be red like crimson, they shall be as wool" (Isaiah 1:18).

2.   THE GOD OF ISAIAH
Isaiah 1:18

Isaiah's majestic book begins with an invitation in verse 18. As always, the invitation is from God to sinful men. It was God who sought Adam in the Garden of Eden with the question, "Adam where art thou?" The great God of the universe is shown by Isaiah to be a God who is interested in each individual man. This God is seen here:

I. PLEADING with the Sinner.
    A.   With *urgency,* "come now."
    B.   With *understanding,* "let us reason together."

II. PICTURING the Sinner's Sin (which is):
    A.   *Deeply imbedded,* "scarlet."
    B.   *Dangerously inflaming,* "scarlet."

III. PURGING the Sinner.
    A.   Resulting in *purity,* "snow."
    B.   Resulting in *peace,* "wool."
        1. Peace through the blood of the Lamb. Colossians 1:20.
        2. Clothed with the righteousness of the same Lamb.

The invitation here extended by God is still open today. The Lord Jesus Christ promises, "him that cometh to me I will in no wise cast out" (John 6:37b). Will you come?

3. WHEN MEN BECOME MICE
Isaiah 2:12-22

"Are you a man or a mouse? Squeak up!" How many times have you heard that humorous expression? Actually a man never becomes a mouse. But we refer to indecisive, cowardly men as mice. Isaiah reveals that a day is coming in which the false façade of man's pride and strength is going to be torn away, and men will face the judgment of God. Man's external display of confidence will then disappear, and those who once prided themselves in being self-sufficient men will act like "mice." "The day of the Lord of Hosts" will make men tremble before God "for fear of the Lord, and for the glory of His majesty" (Isaiah 2:19, 21). What will happen to men in that Day?

I. Their HUSTLED UP REPUTATIONS Will Be Useless. Isaiah 2:17
   A. The lofty will be lowered.
   B. The haughty will be humbled.
   C. The Lord alone shall be exalted.
   D. "Pride goeth before destruction, and an haughty spirit before a fall" (Proverbs 16:18).

II. Their HOME MADE RELIGIONS Will Be Powerless. Isaiah 2:18
   A. Idolatry is an insult to God.
   B. Allegiance to idols is an affront to God.
   C. Devotion to idols is desecration of God's Law.
   D. Of these home-made religionists, the Apostle Paul writes: "Having a form of godliness, but denying the power thereof: from such turn away" (II Timothy 3:5).

III. Their HOARDED-UP RESOURCES Will Be Worthless. Isaiah 2:7, 20, 21
   A. Silver and gold cannot obtain redemption. I Peter 1:18
   B. Money cannot buy satisfaction. I Timothy 6:6-11
   C. Wealth cannot produce proper worship. Revelation 3:17-19

What meaneth all of this? Isaiah replies, "Cease ye from man, whose breath is in his nostrils: for wherein is he to be accounted of?" (Isaiah 2:22). We must not trust in man nor in man's resources for our salvation. Salvation is of the Lord.

4. A PARALYZING SUBTRACTION
Isaiah 3:1-4

It has been said that men and nations generally get the type of government and leaders they deserve. This is true also in the spiritual realm. Isaiah revealed to Israel that as their nation declined, true men of God would become scarce. Amos put it this way: "Behold, the days come, saith the Lord God, that I will send a famine in the land, not a famine of bread, nor a thirst for water, but of hearing the words of the Lord" (Amos 8:11). The Apostle Paul declares the same truth concerning the "last days." He says: "For the time will come when they will not endure sound doctrine; but after their own lusts shall they heap to themselves teachers, having itching ears; and they shall turn away their ears from the truth, and shall be turned into fables" (II Timothy 4:3, 4). Paul tells us these people obtained the kind of teachers they wanted and deserved. Isaiah prophesies that the same thing is to happen to Israel. How we need to profit from their sad experience! This message will apply the facts of Isaiah's day to the spiritual truths of our day.

I. MEN OF WAR Will Be Lacking in the Latter Days.
   A. "The mighty man," "the man of war," "the captain of fifty." Isaiah 3:2, 3
   B. Few are set for the "defense of the gospel" as was Paul. Philippians 1:17
   C. Few "earnestly contend for the faith" as did Jude. Jude 3
   D. Few have on "the whole armor of God." Ephesians 6:10-18

II. MEN OF DISCERNMENT Will Be Lacking in the Latter Days.
   A. "The judge," "the prudent," "the ancient," "the counsellor." Isaiah 3:2, 3
   B. We are commanded by John to "try the spirits." I John 4:1
   C. We are enjoined by Paul to "prove all things." I Thessalonians 5:21

III. MEN OF LEADERSHIP Will Be Lacking in the Latter Days.
   A. "The prophet . . . the honorable man . . . the cunning artificer . . . and the eloquent orator." Isaiah 3:2, 3
   B. Too many men are like Barak who could not take

charge of the army unless he had Deborah around to instruct him.

C. Too many are like King Saul who refused to exert his sacred right of leadership in the face of Goliath's threats.

How we Christians need to pray that God will give us Men of War, Men of Discernment, and Men of Leadership. Then pray for grace to heed them!

5. SEVEN WOMEN AFTER ONE MAN
Isaiah 4:1-6

This time of tribulation which Isaiah describes in these verses is a solemn illustration of how wide-reaching are the effects of sin and of how complete are the judgments of God on that sin. This passage preaches eloquently the truth of Numbers 32:23: "Be sure your sin will find you out."

I. Sin Brings TRAGEDY to the INDIVIDUAL.
- A. These seven heartbroken widows or "sweethearts" show that no man can sin in a vacuum. Isaiah 4:1
- B. This destruction of man-power illustrates how sin cuts down individuals in their prime. Isaiah 3:25, 26
- C. This situation described by Isaiah proves that God does deal with the sins of individuals.

II. Sin Brings TORMENT to the FAMILY.
- A. Fathers lead their children toward heaven or hell.
- B. Mothers influence either for righteousness or rioting.
- C. King David knew only too well how sin torments a family.
- D. The rich man in hell realized too late just how damaging his evil influence had been on his five brothers. Luke 16:27, 28
- E. Mother Eve lived to see her first-born son murder his brother and thus she saw the fruitage of sin.
- F. The modern breakdown of home-life is the result of sin.

III. Sin Brings TURMOIL to NATIONS.
- A. Sin is a *reproach* to a nation. Proverbs 14:34
- B. Sin brings *ruin* to a nation. Isaiah 3:26
- C. Sin brings the retribution of God on a nation.

The dust of centuries blows over the ruins of nations that forgot God. But let us not forget that nations are made up of individuals, and the way of the transgressor is hard. There is only one remedy for the sin of a nation or an individual, and that remedy is the Lord Jesus Christ. Isaiah tells us that "he that remaineth in Jerusalem shall be called holy. . . . : When the Lord shall have washed away the filth of the daughters of Zion." That was their remedy, and that alone is your remedy for sin.

6. THE MOUTH OF HELL
Isaiah 5:14-16

Hell is and always has been an unpopular subject with the masses of earth's population. However, it is needful to think upon this subject and to do something about averting an eternity of punishment. Wise men always prepare for the inevitable, and it is inevitable that we must die, "and after this, the judgment" (Hebrews 9:27). Christ came to save us from hell. Jesus Christ taught the reality of hell with a heart of compassion, and He died to save men from it. Isaiah opens the mysterious curtains of eternity in these verses before us and gives us an unusual glimpse of Hell.

I. Hell's DIMENSIONS. Isaiah 5:14a
   - A. Measureless.
   - B. Bottomless. Revelation 20:3
   - C. Insatiable. Proverbs 27:20

II. Hell's DEVASTATION. Isaiah 5:14b
   - A. Man's marvels ("glory").
   - B. Man's majority ("multitude").
   - C. Man's majesty ("pomp").
   - D. Man's merriment ("rejoiceth").

III. Hell's DOMINIONS. Isaiah 5:15
   - A. The poor man ("the mean man").
   - B. The powerful man ("mighty man").
   - C. The proud man ("the lofty").
   - D. No partiality.

IV. Hell's DECLARATIONS. Isaiah 5:16
   - A. God is exalted in judgment.
   - B. God is holy.
   - C. God is sanctified in righteousness.

How all-important to escape the place which we have described. The Lord Jesus Christ, knowing how terrible is hell, said: "If thy hand offend thee, cut it off: it is better for thee to enter into life maimed, than having two hands to go into hell, into the fire that shall never be quenched" (Mark 9:43). "Whosoever shall call upon the name of the Lord shall be saved." Do so now!

7. A SUCCESSFUL FAILURE
Isaiah 6:9-13

In the verses before us Isaiah has been commissioned by God to what appears to be a totally fruitless ministry. In this day when pastors are judged by the size of their church memberships, when evangelists are judged by the size of the crowds they attract, it is quite unique to read about such a call and commission as that given to Isaiah. II Corinthians 2:15, 16: "For we are unto God a sweet savour of Christ, in them that are saved, and in them that perish: To the one we are the savour of death unto death; and to the other the savour of life unto life. And who is sufficient for these things?" Isaiah's task was indeed a difficult one. Perhaps you are laboring in a hard place. Then take heart from Isaiah! What is involved in being a "savour of death unto death" or a successful failure?

I. The DULLNESS of the CONDEMNED. Isaiah 6:9, 10
  A. Emotions that are *unresponsive* to the Spirit.
  B. Ears that are *inattentive* to the preaching of the Word.
  C. Eyes that are *unbelieving* concerning the mercy of God.

II. The DURATION of the CHASTISEMENT. Isaiah 6:11, 12
  A. Until men reap what they sow. Galatians 6:8
  B. Until sin pays its wages. Romans 6:23
  C. Until unbelief commits eternal suicide. Isaiah 6:12

III. The DELIVERANCE of the CHOSEN. Isaiah 6:13
  A. Isaiah's ministry *tested* by the dullness.
  B. Isaiah's endurance *toughened* by the duration.
  C. Isaiah's faith *triumphant* because of the assurance of deliverance.
  D. The remnant *testified* to the rewarding grace of God to Isaiah.

Let us remember as we serve the Lord Jesus Christ that the way will not always be easy. The message of the gospel will not always be met with joy. Our experience will be similar to that of the Apostle Paul's in Rome: "And some believed the things which were spoken, and some believed not" (Acts 28:24). But let us be faithful as was Isaiah, and God will reward us with a remnant who will testify to God's wondrous grace!

8. SHAVING WITH A BORROWED RAZOR
Isaiah 7:17-20

Ezekiel 5:1-8 is a key to the meaning of Isaiah's use of the phrase "shave with a razor." Shaving with a razor denotes thorough judgment by God upon His sinning people. Ezekiel's explanation is summed up by the words of the Lord as found in Ezekiel 5:8: "Behold, I, even I, am against thee; and will execute judgments in the midst of thee in the sight of the nations." The razor is a reference to God's instrument of judgment. A "hired" or "borrowed" razor refers to that fact that God would use another nation as His means of punishing His own people for their sin. The passage before us from Isaiah trumpets the truth of God's concern over His erring people. God's methods of judgment teach us that:

I. HUMAN INSTRUMENTS Are Sometimes Used by God. Isaiah 7:17-20
   A. God judges faithlessness such as Ahaz displayed.
   B. God is utterly thorough as shown by the example of shaving.
   C. God is unerringly true in His judgment.
   D. God "makes the wrath of man to praise him" by using the evil machinations of a wicked king to His own sovereign purpose.

II. HOPEFUL INSTITUTIONS Are Often Confounded by God.
   A. The Tower of Babel is an example of this. Genesis 11
   B. The now defunct League of Nations is an example of this. Men put their trust in themselves instead of God, and this always ends in confusion.
   C. The proposed alliance of Ahaz with Assyria shows this. II Chronicles 28:19-22

III. HUMILIATING INSOLENCE Is Sometimes Allowed by God.
   A. Example of Samson grinding in the prison house. Judges 16:21
   B. Example of David and Absalom's insolence to him. I Samuel 16:22
   C. Example of Saul and Jonathan falling to the Philistines who made sport of their remains. I Samuel 31:12, 13

Someone has said that "the mills of God grind slowly but they grind exceedingly fine." How we need to walk in obedience to God realizing that "it is a fearful thing to fall into the hands of the living God" (Hebrews 10:31).

9. PEEPING AND MUTTERING IN THE DARK
Isaiah 8:19-22

The world is full of "spiritists" and "wizards" who are "peeping" and "muttering" when what we really need are men who have as their authority the "Thus saith the Lord" of the Bible. Paul's admonition to Timothy is still applicable to preachers today: "Preach the Word!" The Bible is not suffering from lack of proof of its authenticity; it is suffering from lack of proclamation of its assurances. To deny the Bible its place in our lives is to deprive ourselves of the Bread of Life.

I. Bible-deniers Have DARKNESS for LIGHT.
   A. Isaiah 8:20: "If they speak not according to this word, it is because there is no light in them." See Matthew 6:23.
   B. They are in the dark about eternity past.
      1. No light have they on creation.
      2. No light have they on the reason for man's futile history.
   C. They are in the dark about the present earthly turmoil.
      1. They blame their troubles on everything but sin.
      2. They reject the one cure for their troubles — Christ.
   D. They are in the dark about the future eternity.

II. Bible-deniers Have STARVATION for NOURISHMENT. Isaiah 8:21
   A. Physical sufficiency cannot feed the soul. Luke 12:19
   B. Intellectual accomplishment cannot satisfy the soul and its longings. Ecclesiastes 1:16-18

III. Bible-deniers Have DELUSION for HOPE. Isaiah 8:22 The Lord Jesus Christ describes this in Luke 21:25, 26
   A. Nations in confusion.
   B. Nature in convulsion.
   C. Men in consternation.

Truly, "Thy Word is a lamp unto my feet, and a light unto my path" (Psalm 119:105). How we need that Word today! How we need the light of that lamp! How we need the beacon of that light! May God grant us grace to walk in the light of His Word.

10. THE ZEAL OF THE LORD
Isaiah 9:7

The future earthly reign of the Lord Jesus Christ is predicted in Isaiah 9:7. This kingdom is to be characterized by unending peace and "justice from henceforth even forever." That is a big order! How can all of this be accomplished? Isaiah's answer — "The zeal of the Lord of hosts will perform this."

"Zeal" comes from the same Hebrew root as does the word "jealousy." Webster defines "zeal" as "ardor in the pursuit of anything; ardent and active interest; enthusiasm; fervor." The zeal of the Lord is enthusiasm personified. It is active interest hitched to omnipotence. The zeal of the Lord is fervor mightily motivated by holy jealousy. The zeal of the Lord will accomplish a universal peace because of this zeal's allies. Man's zeal often fails because of its lack of supporting strength. It is sometimes said of a very zealous person, "He has a ton of zeal and an ounce of sense." Not so with the Lord. His zeal is effective because:

I. His Zeal Is Governed by ETERNAL WISDOM.
   A. This wisdom was shown in the *creation* of the world. Proverbs 3:19
   B. This wisdom was shown in the *calling* of the disciples.
      1. Christ knew there could be diversity in unity.
      2. Christ knew the Body was not one member but many members. I Corinthians 12:12-18
   C. This wisdom will be shown in the *conduct* of His Kingdom.

II. His Zeal Is Backed Up by ENDLESS WEALTH.
   A. Many good causes and purposes go into oblivion because of lack of funds.
   B. But the Messiah's *income* is infinite. Psalm 50:10-12
   C. The Messiah's *inheritance* is universal. Psalm 2:8

III. His Zeal Is Backed Up by EFFECTUAL WEAPONS.
   A. The "rod of iron" says His power is *irresistible*. Psalm 2:9
   B. "Twelve legions of angels" suggests that His hosts are *innumerable*. Matthew 26:53
   C. Revelation 19:11-16 indicates His forces to be *indestructible*.

Certainly our zeal ought to be channeled into the proclamation of the gospel of Him who shall someday be King of kings and Lord of lords.

11. BOASTING EXCLUDED
Isaiah 10:15

Isaiah 10 tells of God's impending judgment upon Assyria for her pride and injustice. God had used Assyria to punish Samaria, but the Assyrians had grown conceited and cruel in their accomplishments. They became drunk with power and boasted of their strength as though they were self-sufficient and God was non-existent. God despises boasting and pride. His hatred of this sin is as much so today as it was in Isaiah's day, and we need to guard against the sin of boastfulness. In II Timothy 3:2 Paul warns us that in the "perilous times" of the "last days" men shall be "boasters." In the Christian life, we might ask with the Apostle Paul, "Where is boasting then?" We need also to give the answer of the Apostle, "It is excluded" (Romans 3:27). Boasting should be excluded:

I. In the Matter of STEWARDSHIP.

    A. Paul *expresses* it. "And what hast thou that thou didst not receive? now if thou didst receive it, why dost thou glory, as if thou hast not received it?" (I Corinthians 4:7).

    B. James *emphasizes* it. "Every good gift and every perfect gift is from above, and cometh down from the Father above . . ." (James 1:17).

    C. Paul *explains* it. "Moreover it is required in stewards, that a man be found *faithful*" (I Corinthians 4:2) *not boastful.*

II. In the Matter of SERVICE.

    A. "So likewise ye, when ye shall have done all those things which are commanded you, say, We are unprofitable servants: we have done that which was our duty to do" (Luke 17:10).

    B. In the light of Calvary we are *duty-bound* to serve.

    C. In view of a lost world we are *debtors.* Romans 1:14

III. In the Matter of SALVATION. Romans 3:27

    A. Salvation is a gift, not a paycheck. Ephesians 2:8, 9

    B. The Saviour is THE One of whom to boast. Said the Psalmist, "My soul shall make her boast in the Lord" (Psalm 34:2).

May we say with the Apostle Paul: "He that glorieth, let him glory in the Lord" (I Corinthians 1:31).

12. A DESCRIPTION OF THE MILLENNIUM
Isaiah 11:1-9

There have been men in every generation who have envisioned an earthly utopia where all would be peace and righteousness. Always these dreams have been dashed upon the rocks of man's sin, selfishness, and stupidity. The Word of God reveals that such a time will come but only when the Lord Jesus Christ, the Prince of Peace, comes to this earth the second time. His coming will be spectacular and truly revolutionary. His reign will bring universal peace and flawless judgment and righteousness. Isaiah describes what this millennial reign will bring to this earth. We call this rule of Christ the "millennium" because Revelation 20:4-6 reveals to us that this universal reign of Christ will last for one thousand years, after which the White Throne Judgment will take place. Then we will go on into eternity. Let us examine Isaiah's account of the millennium.

I. The PEERLESS CHRIST and His CHARACTER. Isaiah 11:3-5
   A. Unerring judgment. 11:3
   B. Unwavering discipline. 11:4
   C. Untarnished righteousness. 11:5
   D. Unfaltering faithfulness. 11:5
   E. HE is the Alpha and the Omega. He is the Apple of God's eye, the Bread of Life, the Chiefest of Ten Thousand, the Deliverer of souls, the Excellency of glory, the Firm Foundation of the church, the Gift of God, the Highly Honored One, the Immanuel, the Judge of all the earth, the King of kings, the Life, the Magnificence of Majesty, the Name above all names, the Offering for sin, the great Physician, the Quickening Spirit, the Rose of Sharon, the Good Shepherd, the Truth, the Upholder of all things, the Victory, the Way to heaven, the Exalted One, the Yahweh of the Old Testament, and the Zealous One. HE is All in all.

II. The PEACEFUL CREATION and Its CONDITION. Isaiah 11:6-8
   A. The curse will be lifted from nature. 11:6
   B. The animal creation will be tame and harmless. 11:7
   C. The poison of sin will be gone. 11:8

III. The PERFECT CIVILIZATION and Its COMPLETE-
NESS. Isaiah 11:9
A. Culture will have Christ at its center.
B. Education will have the "knowledge of the Lord" as
its sum.
C. Government will have Christ the King as its executive.

13.   THE WELLS OF SALVATION
Isaiah 12:3

"Therefore with joy shall ye draw water out of the wells of salvation." With these words the Prophet Isaiah glories in the resources of God's "so great salvation." This verse reminds us of the Feast of Tabernacles as told in John 7 when Jesus, the Water of Life, stood up and declared: "If any man thirst, let him come unto me, and drink. He that believeth on me, as the Scripture hath said, out of his belly shall flow rivers of living water" (John 7:37, 38). Just what are the wells that produce this Water of Life?

I. The Well of God's LOVE.
  A.   God's love *offered up* His Son. John 3:16
  B.   God's love *overcomes* our unloveliness. I John 4:10, 19
  C.   God's love *overflows* all boundaries. Ephesians 2:17-19
   1. So *wide* that it removes "our transgressions from us" "as far as the east is from the west" (Psalm 103:12).
   2. So *long* that God testifies: "I have loved thee with an everlasting love: therefore with lovingkindness have I drawn thee" (Jeremiah 31:3).
   3. So *deep* that He has buried our sins in "the depths of the sea" (Micah 7:19).
   4. So *high* that "He stretcheth out the north over the empty place, and hangeth the earth upon nothing. He bindeth up the waters in his thick clouds" (Job 26:7, 8).

II. The Well of God's PEACE.
  A.   *Saving* peace. Romans 5:1
  B.   *Steadfast* peace. Philippians 4:6, 7
  C.   *Satisfying* peace. Isaiah 26:3

III. The Well of God's FORGIVENESS.
  A.   Peter preached it. Acts 5:29-31
  B.   Paul proclaimed it. Acts 13:38, 39

IV. The Well of God's RIGHTEOUSNESS. Romans 3:21; II Corinthians 5:21.

Will you not drink deeply from the wells of salvation today? Isaiah promises joy to the one who so drinks!

14. CORRUPTION, CONFUSION AND CONDEMNATION
Isaiah 13:1-22

The word translated "Babylon" has the meaning of "confusion." This word is found in Genesis 11 where the Lord confounded the language of all the earth. The monument to man's pride was there called the Tower of Babel, or Confusion. In the thirteenth chapter of Isaiah God deals with the literal Babylon then existing in Isaiah's time, but I believe there is also a greater prophetic meaning, especially from verse 12 on. The Babylon described in verses 12 thru 22 is a picture of what is shown in Revelation 17 and 18. The literal Babylon of Isaiah's day, the religious Babylon of Revelation, and the commerical Babylon of Revelation are our subjects of consideration in this message. Each of these Babylons proves that the corruption of sin leads to confusion, and finally to the condemnation of God's wrath.

I. The Babylon of Isaiah's day — A CORRUPTED CITY. Isaiah 13:1-11
   A. *Corrupted* through iniquity and evil, "arrogancy of the proud" and "haughtiness of the terrible." Isaiah 13:11
   B. *Confusion* her lot because of her sin. Isaiah 13:7, 8
   C. *Condemned* by God. Isaiah 13:9

II. The Religious Babylon — A COUNTERFEIT CHRISTIANITY. Revelation 17:1-16
   A. Religion is *corrupted* by compromise with the world. 17:1, 2
   B. Corrupt religion is *confounded* by the nations. 17:15, 16
   C. Corrupt religion is *condemned* by God. 17:17, 18

III. The Commercial Babylon — A COLOSSAL CORPORATION. Revelation 18:1-19
   A. *Championed* by evil men. Revelation 18:3
   B. *Condemned* by an Holy God. Revelation 18:5, 6
   C. *Crushed* by an Almighty God. Revelation 18:8

What Isaiah pictures and the Revelation portrays is what this Christ-rejecting world is coming to. Only the supernatural power of Christ the King will put an end to the confusion in which men and nations find themselves. Only the Prince of Peace can deliver this world from its self-created chaos. How we need to pray with John, "Even so, come, Lord Jesus."

15. WHEN THE TABLES ARE TURNED
Isaiah 14:1-17

Isaiah 14 is a story or stories of "the tables being turned." Later on in history Ezekiel proclaims the same type of message when he writes: ". . . when iniquity shall have an end . . . exalt him that is low, and abase him that is high. I will overturn, overturn, overturn it: and it shall be no more, until he come whose right it is: and I will give it him" (Ezekiel 21:25-27). The Lord Jesus Christ also preached a similar message. He said: "So the last shall be first, and the first last: for many be called, but few chosen" (Matthew 20:16). What does all of this mean? It means that a day is coming when God is going to set things right. To do so a great many things are going to have to be turned upside-down, as we say. The tables are going to be turned:

I. On Satan-inspired Peoples. Isaiah 14:4-11
   A. The strength of the wicked will become weakness. 14:5, 10
   B. The riches of the wicked will become poverty. 14:4, 9; Luke 16:25
   C. The music of the wicked will become mourning. 14:6, 11

II. On Satan Himself. Isaiah 14:12-17
   A. Lucifer, Son of Morning, became the Prince of the Powers of Darkness.
   B. He who sought to ascend the high places of heaven will be locked in the bottomless pit. Revelation 20:3
   C. He who desired to be a king above God will forever be the Prisoner of God. Revelation 20:10

III. On Christians! Yes, the tables are even going to be turned for Christians. Isaiah promised God's people deliverance in 14:1-3. There are two kinds of Christians, and for both of these the tables will turn.
   A. For the "shirkers" (carnal Christians). ". . . wood, hay, stubble. . . . If any man's work shall be burned, he shall suffer loss: but he himself shall be saved; yet so as by fire" (I Corinthians 3:12-15).
   B. For the workers (Spiritual Christians). "Blessed are they that mourn: for they shall be comforted . . ." (Matthew 5:4-12).

Yes, someday the Lord Jesus Christ is going to make all things what they should be and set everything in its proper perspective. Let us live with this in mind.

16. WEEPING IN THE NIGHT
Isaiah 15:1-9

Sin and darkness go together. Sin casts shadows of sorrow wherever its murky figure goes. Sin snatches the sparkle of innocence from the youthful eye and plucks the flower of purity from the dimpled cheek of a smiling maiden. Sin blinds the eyes of men to the destruction hidden within the so-called "harmless" pleasures of this world. In this fifteenth chapter of Isaiah, the Prophet records for us the sorrow and remorse of Moab — heartbreak which is a direct result of sin. Twelve times in this chapter Isaiah tells of the sorrow that has befallen Moab with the verbs "weep," "howl," and "cry." Sin always brings sorrow and weeping. Sin always brings darkness, spiritually, intellectually and morally. Sin also brings:

I. The DARKNESS of DENIAL. Luke 22:59-62
   A. Peter's denial was the result of an *emphasis on self*.
   B. Peter's denial was the result of the *exclusion* of watchful *supplication*.
   C. Peter's denial ended in *weeping in the night*.
   D. Christian, denying of Christ always ends in heartbreak.

II. The DARKNESS of DEATH. Romans 6:23
   A. Isaiah 15:9 summarizes death's tragic triumph over Moab: "For the waters of Dimon shall be full of blood."
   B. Physical death is the result of sin. Romans 5:12
   C. Eternal death is the awful penalty of sin. Revelation 20:15

III. The DARKNESS of DESTRUCTION. Isaiah 15:5-9
   A. Sin destroys *peace*. Nimrim, in verse 6, was a place of well-watered gardens and speaks of peace.
   B. Sin destroys *productivity*. 15:6, "there is no green thing."
   C. Sin destroys *prosperity*. 15:7, "the abundance . . . shall they carry away."
   D. No wonder, then, that "the cry is gone round about the borders of Moab." Isaiah 15:8

Repent of your sin today. "For godly sorrow worketh repentance to salvation not to be repented of: but the sorrow of the world worketh death" (II Corinthians 7:10) and weeping in the night of despair.

17. WANDERING BIRDS
Isaiah 16:2

"For it shall be, that, as a wandering bird cast out of the nest, so the daughters of Moab shall be at the fords of Arnon." In this chapter (16) Isaiah continues his record of "The burden of Moab." The Moabites are a picture of all sinners — they are pictured as wanderers. Sinners are individuals who are "Drifting with no port in sight." Isaiah refers to these Moabites as "wandering birds." In this message we would have you see the costliness of being a "wanderer."

I. The Sinner Is WANDERING from the SHEPHERD. Isaiah 53:6, "All we like sheep have gone astray. . . ."
   A. The wandering sheep has *no Pilot* to guide it.
   B. The wandering sheep has *no Provider* to feed it.
   C. The wandering sheep has *no Protector* to guard it.
   D. How much better to be able to say: "The Lord is my Shepherd; I shall not want" (Psalm 23:1).

II. The Sinner Is WASTING His SUBSTANCE. Luke 15:13 ". . . wasted his substance with riotous living."
   A. A sinner wastes his intellect on vanity.
   B. A sinner spends his energy on that which is temporal.
   C. A sinner consumes his time at the expense of eternal values.
   D. A sinner uses his influence for that which destroys.
   E. How much better to "present your bodies a living sacrifice, holy, acceptable unto God . . ." (Romans 12:1).

III. The Sinner Is WANTING SHELTER. Psalm 11:1 ". . . how say ye to my soul, Flee as a bird to your mountain?"
   A. The wanderer has no place of *refuge*.
   B. The wanderer has no place of *restoration*.
   C. The wanderer has no place for *rest*.
   D. How much better to be able to say to God: "Thou art my rock and my fortress" (Psalm 31:3).

Wanderer, come home! Jesus invites you: "Come unto me, all ye that labor and are heavy laden, and I will give you rest" (Matthew 11:28).

18.   RESPECTABLE EYESIGHT
Isaiah 17:7-11

"At that day shall a man look to his Maker, and his eyes shall have respect to the Holy One of Israel. And he shall not look to the altars, the work of his hands, neither shall respect that which his fingers have made, either the groves, or the images." In these words Isaiah discusses eyesight which has *respect* to the "Holy One of Israel." In this message we want to discuss the Christian's spiritual sight along three lines, for if there was ever a day when we need good eyesight, it is the day in which we live. Isaiah promises that we shall someday see our "Maker." How can we properly prepare ourselves for this meeting with God?

I.   HINDSIGHT Is *Advantageous* to *Saints*.
    A.   *Remember* the *pit* from which we have been brought. Psalm 40:2
    B.   *Recall* the *poverty* from which we have been saved. Psalm 34:6; Isaiah 17:10, 11
    C.   *Review* the *perils* through which we have come.
        The song writer says:
        "Thro' many danger, toils, and snares,
        I have already come.
        'Tis grace hath bro't me safe thus far,
        And grace will lead me home."

II.   PRESENT SIGHT Is *Admonished* in *Scripture*.
    A.   Look to yourselves. II John 8
    B.   Look to Jesus. Hebrews 12:2
    C.   Look upon the harvest fields. John 4:35
    D.   Look into the Word of God. James 1:25

III.   FORESIGHT Is *Analyzed* by the *Seer*. Isaiah 17:7-11
    A.   Our *respect* will be *occupied* with the Almighty.
    B.   Our *religion* will be *obliterated*. "he shall not look to the altars" (Isaiah 17:8a).
    C.   Our *righteousnesses* will be *overshadowed*. "the work of his hands."

"Hindsight *is* too often better than foresight." But as we allow the Word of God to guide our thinking, may we be accurate in our foresight as was Moses who "endured, as seeing him who is invisible" (Hebrews 11:27).

19. SOUR GRAPES AND PRUNING HOOKS
Isaiah 18:1-7

False security and carnal complacency characterize our generation. Such was also the case with the Ethiopians of whom Isaiah prophesies. They were a people given to worldly pursuits and earthly ends. Their judgment ought to be a sober lesson to us today.

  I. The CARELESSNESS of the Ethiopians. Isaiah 18:1, 2
  - A. Trusting in military *might*, "shadowing with wings."
  - B. Trusting in political *machinations*, "sendeth ambassadors."
  - C. Trusting in self-centered *materialism*.

  II. The CONCENTRATION of God's Judgment. Isaiah 18:3-6
  - A. As a *picture* to the world. 18:3
  - B. As a *punishment* to the Ethiopians. 18:4-6
  - C. As a *proof* of God's righteous power.

  III. The CONSUMMATION of God's Purpose. Isaiah 18:7
  - A. God's *person honored*, "unto the Lord."
  - B. God's *people humbled*, "a people scattered."
  - C. God's *place hallowed*, "to the place . . . the mount Zion."

The pruning hooks of God's chastisement are sure and accurate. Before man can realize his selfish dreams and bring to pass his carnal imaginations, God will cut him off in judgment and retribution. God's people alone are really safe and secure. Only God's people are truly fruitful and eternally prosperous.

20. EGYPT'S FINAL DESTINY
Isaiah 19:1-25

In Bible typology Egypt is a picture of the world. In this nineteenth chapter of Isaiah is portrayed for us the final destiny of this nation. We believe that Isaiah's prophecy will be literally fulfilled and that Egypt as a nation will see her history culminate exactly as Isaiah has predicted. But since Egypt is a picture of the world, her final destiny is also a picture of the world's final destiny, generally speaking. The same seeds of destruction and disaster which come to fruition in Egypt's humiliation are present in all of the great world powers of this age. Men are trusting their weapons of warfare and their intellectual ingenuity, but all of their fortresses will crumble before the awesome revelation of God's power. Let us study Isaiah's blueprint for Egypt's and the world's final destiny.

I. The FAILURE of Worldly DEFENSES. Isaiah 19:1-7
   A. Their *relationships* will be *confounded.* 19:1-3
   B. Their *ruler* will be *cruel.* 19:4
   C. Their *resources* will be *cursed.* 19:5-7

II. The FUTILITY of Worldly DEVICES. Isaiah 19:8-16
   A. Their *ambitions* will be *upset.* 19:8-10
   B. Their *advisers* will be *useless.* 19:11-13
   C. Their *actions* will be *undermined.* 19:14-16

III. The FAITHFULNESS of God's DETERMINATIONS. Isaiah 19:17-25.
   A. *Devotion* to God will be *rendered.* 19:17-19
   B. *Deliverance* by God will be *revealed.* 19:20-22
   C. *Delight* in Israel will be *restored.* 19:23-25

The failure and futility of the world's greatest accomplishments remind us of I John 2:16, 17: "For all that is in the world, the lust of the flesh, and the lust of the eyes, and the pride of life, is not of the Father, but is of the world. And the world passeth away, and the lust thereof: but he that doeth the will of God abideth forever."

21. BOLD HUMILITY
Isaiah 20:1-6

The Christian life is full of seeming paradoxes. We are dead yet alive. We are weak but strong. We are poor yet rich. And we are to be humble yet bold. Holy boldness is needed today as never before. The believer who is faithful to God will experience humiliation sometimes, but Isaiah is an example of God's blessing upon those who are willing to be what God desires them to be.

I. OBEDIENCE to God Demands BRAVE HUMILITY.
  A. Isaiah accepted God's *requirement*.
  B. Isaiah endured the *reproach* it brought. Hebrews 13:13
  C. Isaiah warned of the *results* of compromise.
  D. Isaiah will reap the *reward* of an obedient prophet.

II. OPPOSITION from the World Causes BURNING HUMILIATION.
  A. Isaiah experienced this.
  B. New Testament saints endured this.
    1. Peter and John were imprisoned.
    2. Paul was publicly whipped.
    3. John was exiled on Patmos.
    4. I Corinthians 4:8-13.

III. OFFENSIVENESS of the Message Requires BOLD HUMILITY.
  A. Sometimes offends *pride* of individuals.
  B. Sometimes offends *politics* of nations.
  C. Sometimes offends *programs* of churches.

Isaiah's task as outlined in this twentieth chapter was certainly no easy one. But neither is the job of the faithful believer. We can be sure, however, that the same God who took care of Isaiah will also give us sufficient grace to obey Him.

22. WATCHMAN, WHAT OF THE NIGHT?
Isaiah 21:11, 12

We live in an age of darkness. Moral darkness, spiritual darkness, political darkness, and social darkness are descending upon the scenes of this world. Believers are called to be lights in this darkened world of sin. We are commanded to Watch and Pray. Isaiah asks a very probing question, "Watchman, What of the Night?" Let us examine that question in this message.

I. The RESPONSIBILITY of the Watchman.
   A. To be *awake*. I Corinthians 15:34
   B. To be *alert*. I Peter 5:8
   C. To be *accountable*. II Corinthians 5:10

II. The REASON for the Night.
   A. *Rebellion* against the *Scriptures*. Isaiah 8:20
   B. *Rejection* of the *Son*. John 8:12
   C. *Reveling* in *sin*. John 3:19; I Thessalonians 5:7

III. The RESPONSE of the Watchman, Isaiah 21:12
   A. The *incentive*, "the morning cometh and also the night."
   B. The *inquiry*. Hebrews 2:3
   C. The *invitation*, "return, come."

The Watchman must give the message that the "morning cometh" BUT ALSO "the night." For some, the coming of Christ means the brightness of eternal morning. For the unsaved, the coming of Christ only brings with it the reality of outer darkness and eternal loss. What the individual does with the Light of the World, Jesus Christ, determines which it shall be for him.

23. A BOUNCING BALL
Isaiah 22:18, 19

The Israelites had become quite complacent in their lethargic attitude toward the message of God's prophets. They were satisfied to think they were safe and secure. But Isaiah tells them that the judgment of God will fall, and God "will surely turn and toss thee like a ball into a large country: there shalt thou die." Many folks feel that their "sphere" of activity is all-important. Why worry about the "hereafter" they ask. But God warns us to turn from our wicked preoccupation with this world and look to eternal things. Abraham was commended because "he looked for a city which hath foundations, whose builder and maker is God" (Hebrews 11:10). Judgment is so sudden. It is like a ball that is bounced — the ball is helpless in the hand of the one tossing it. So is man in the hand of an omnipotent God.

I. Bounced from TIME INTO ETERNITY.
   - A. Death is *sure.*
   - B. Death is often *sudden.*
   - C. Death is always *separation.*

II. Bounced from GLORY INTO SHAME.
   - A. Pride goeth before a *fall.*
   - B. Pride often loses its *friends.* (Example of Prodigal Son)
   - C. Pride bears a terrible *fruit.* Proverbs 11:2

III. Bounced from PLENTY TO POVERTY.
   - A. Illustrated in Luke 16:19-23
   - B. Impelled by God. v. 19 — "I will drive thee"
   - C. Irrevocable thru eternity.

Heed Paul's exhortation in Colossians 3:2: "Set your affection on things above, not on things on the earth."

24. THE CITY THAT WAS MADE AN OBJECT LESSON
Isaiah 23:5-11

The overthrow of Tyre is one of the dramatically great stories of Bible history. Tyre was a proud and prosperous city; a cosmopolitan and commercial city; an enterprising and exalted city. She was also a sinful city. In this twenty-third chapter of Isaiah is described for us the overthrow and restoration (after seventy years) of this mighty, magnificent metropolis. God made Tyre an object lesson to the world. This object lesson proved at least three things about the God who overthrew Tyre.

I. God Alone Is SOVEREIGN.
  A. His person is deserving of our *worship*.
  B. His wisdom is deserving of our *wealth*.
  C. His power is deserving of our *willingness*.

II. God Alone Is SAVIOUR.
  A. *Civilization* cannot *save*. 23:7, "your joyous city."
  B. *Culture* cannot *survive*. "antiquity."
  C. *Corporations* cannot *salvage*. 23:8

III. God Alone Has the SOLUTION.
  A. Pride of man must be *stained*. 23:9
  B. Strength of man must be *sapped*. 23:14
  C. Complacency of man must be *shaken*. 23:11

These three lessons concerning God are vital to our lives. God is on the throne; He is our salvation; He can remedy our lost estate. To turn from Him is disaster; to turn to Him is victory.

25. THE GREAT TRIBULATION DESCRIBED
Isaiah 24:17-23

In this twenty-fourth chapter of his prophecy, Isaiah looks beyond the immediate threat of the Assyrian armies to a distant future day. Isaiah has predicted that God will judge and destroy the proud and mighty legions of the Assyrian hosts, but in this chapter Isaiah describes for the reader how God will someday overthrow all of the great world-powers which set themselves in array against Him. Isaiah's description of the utter chaos prevalent upon the earth immediately before the reign of the Messiah is similar to the description given by John in Revelation, Chapters 6 through 19, in which John unfolds before our eyes the Tribulation Period. This Tribulation Period is the last gasp of a rebellious world. How does Isaiah describe it?

I. THE DEATH RATTLE of a Dying World. Isaiah 24:16, 17, 21

    A. The *fading* of earth's treasures. I John 2:17
        1. The lust of the flesh
        2. The lust for material things.
        3. The lust for fame — "the world passeth away, and the lust thereof."

    B. The *falling* of earth's leaders. Isaiah 24:21; Revelation 6:12-17
        1. Politicians who rejected the King of kings will bow to Him.
        2. Educators who scoffed at the Word of God will see it fulfilled.
        3. Philosophers who sneered at the wisdom of God will know their folly.
        4. Entertainers who laughed at the Light of the World will mourn.

II. The DEFINITIVE REASON for a Dying World. Isaiah 24:5, 6

    A. In the natural realm, men have defiled God's creation.
    B. In the moral realm, men have transgressed God's laws.
    C. In the religious realm, men have perverted His ordinances.
    D. In the universal realm, men have broken His covenant.
    E. Therefore, II Thessalonians 2:8-12 must come to pass.

III. The DESTRUCTIVE RAVAGES Suffered by a Dying
World. Isaiah 24:18-20, 23
   A. Isaiah may refer to nuclear destruction or worse.
   B. Revelation 9:13-21 is akin to Isaiah's prophecy.

IV. The DELIVERER-REDEEMER Is Your Only Hope As a
Dying Sinner. John 3:16

26. HE HAS ALL YOU NEED
Isaiah 25:4

This is an age of tranquilizers and sleeping pills. Many are troubled by economic, emotional and moral problems. All kinds of solutions are proposed, and often the real solution is ignored. The real solution is, of course, the God of the Bible. He has all you need, and you need all He has.

I. A Great SUPPLY for the Poor.
- A. According to the *resources* of His *grace*. Romans 8:32
- B. According to the *riches* in *glory*. Philippians 4:19

II. A Great SOLACE to the Distressed.
- A. Christ Himself has been *tried* in the *flesh*. Hebrew 4:15, 16
- B. He, therefore, can be *touched* with the *feeling* of our infirmity.

III. A Great SHELTER from the Storm.
- A. He is the Rock of Ages.
- B. He is the Haven of Rest.

IV. A Great SHADOW from the Heat.
- A. From the heat of *persecution*.
- B. From the heat of *perdition*.

The Lord Jesus Christ said, "The Spirit of the Lord is upon me, because he hath anointed me to preach the gospel to the poor; he hath sent me to heal the brokenhearted, to preach deliverance to the captives, and recovering of sight to the blind, to set at liberty them that are bruised" (Luke 4:18). Certainly He has all you need, all you need for time and eternity.

27. A FORMULA FOR MENTAL HEALTH
Isaiah 26:3

Between twenty and twenty-five thousand people commit suicide in the United States of America every year. These people have not been able to find the answers to their seemingly insurmountable problems. Peace is the pursuit of nations and individuals, and peace seems to be the most elusive prize of all. The fact is that only the Prince of Peace Himself, Jesus Christ, can give real peace. Isaiah gives us a formula in this verse which will result in peace, perfect peace.

I. The MIGHT of God.

    A. A mighty *promise*, "Thou wilt."
    B. A mighty *power*, "keep."
    C. A mighty *peace*, "perfect peace."

II. The MIND of Man.

    A. Faith has *reason* for *optimism*.
    B. Faith has the *right object*, "on Thee."
    C. Faith has the *rest* of *obedience*.

III. The MINGLING of both.

    "Whose mind is stayed on thee: because he trusteth in thee."
    A. God's *concern* is for man. I Peter 5:7
    B. Man's *confidence* is in God.

If you reject God's formula for peace, you can have no peace. "But the wicked are like the troubled sea, when it cannot rest, whose waters cast up mire and dirt. There is no peace, saith my God, to the wicked" (Isaiah 57:20, 21). "Therefore, being justified by faith, we have peace with God through our Lord Jesus Christ," writes Paul in Romans 5:1. "And the peace of God, which passeth all understanding, shall keep your hearts and minds through Christ Jesus" (Philippians 4:7).

28. GOD'S CONCERN FOR HIS PEOPLE
Isaiah 27:1-13

The Bible pictures our God as a great sovereign Shepherd who lovingly and wisely directs the affairs of His sheep. He has knowledge of the needs of the sheep, of the wiles of the enemies of the sheep, and He also knows the dangerous weaknesses and tendencies of His sheep. But with infinite concern and omnipotent patience He lovingly leads them along. His chosen people, Israel, have had to learn many bitter lessons, but God's promises to them will still be fulfilled. Believers today ought to take heart from this knowledge.

I. God CARES for His People. 27:1-6
   A. This *requires* God's *fury*.
   B. This *reveals* God's *faithfulness*.
   C. This *results* in Israel's *fruitfulness*.

II. God CHASTISES His People. 27:7-11
   A. *Iniquity* necessitates it. 27:9
   B. *Instruction* is involved in it. 27:10
   C. *Ingathering* is its purpose.

III. God CONGREGATES His People. 27:12, 13
   A. God *beats*, "the Lord shall beat."
   B. God *blows*, "the trumpet shall be blown."
   C. God *blesses*, "worship the Lord."

We need to remember the exhortation of the writer of Hebrews: "My son, despise not thou the chastening of the Lord, nor faint when thou art rebuked of him: For whom the Lord loveth he chasteneth, and scourgeth every son whom he receiveth. If ye endure chastening, God dealeth with you as sons; for what son is he whom the father chasteneth not?" (Hebrews 12:5-7).

29. SHORT BEDS AND DRUNKARDS
Isaiah 28:1-20

Alcoholism and drunkenness curse our beloved America. Thousands upon thousands of so-called social drinkers are destined to become hopeless and helpless drunkards. The curse of liquor is evident in every area of our society. There is no stratum of our society that has escaped its evil fruit. Isaiah cries out against this wicked sin, and brings a fearsome indictment against those who are guilty of promoting this evil and against those who are guilty of indulging in it. Listen to this indictment.

I. Drunkenness DEGRADES LEADERSHIP. 28:1-6
   A. Brings the *reproach* of God, "Woe."
   B. Brings the *ruin* of a nation. 28:3, 4

II. Drunkenness DEGENERATES LEARNING. 28:7, 8
   A. Judgment is *perverted*.
   B. Religion is *prostituted*.
   C. Society is *polluted*.

III. Drunkenness DEPENDS on LIES. 28:15
   A. A foolish covenant.
   B. A false complacency.
   C. A failing comfort.

IV. Drunkenness DOOMED by the LINE. 28:17-20
   A. The standard will discover the lack.
   B. The scourge will drive away the lies.
   C. The shortness will divulge the lewdness.

The tragic commentary of Isaiah's day is paralleled by that of our day. It was the religious folks of Isaiah's day who failed to take a stand against this evil, and when God's people fail to stand against an evil, they eventually fall for it. May we take warning from Isaiah's impassioned plea.

30. DELUDED DREAMERS
Isaiah 29:7, 8

The Devil is called the Deceiver. The human heart is deceitful above all things, declares the Bible. Paul prophesied that "evil men and seducers shall wax worse and worse, deceiving, and being deceived" (II Timothy 3:13). We are living in those days. Men are deceived into believing that man's soul can be satisfied with pleasure; that life does consist in the abundance of things which a man possesses. But Isaiah describes the bitter discovery which such deceived people must inevitably make — this world cannot satisfy and man cannot ignore God and win.

I. Hungry Men Dreaming of DINING.
    A. *Stones* instead of bread.
    B. *Shadow* instead of substance.
    C. *Sham* instead of reality.

II. Thirsty Men Dreaming of DRINKING.
    A. The world's fountains are *poisoned*.
    B. The world's springs are *polluted*.
    C. The world's tongues are *parched*.

III. Fighting Men Dreaming of DELIVERING.
    "so shall the multitude of all the nations be, that fight against mount Zion."
    A. Man's wishes against God's weapons.
    B. Man's strategy against God's strength.
    C. Man's mirage against God's majesty.

What is the answer to man's deluded self-deception? "Jesus said unto them, I am the bread of life. He that cometh to me shall never hunger; and he that believeth on me shall never thirst" (John 6:35).

31. SINFUL FAITH
Isaiah 30:1-7

There is a dangerous philosophy which says, "It does not make any difference what you believe just as long as you are sincere." This philosophy is dangerous because it is wrong. Faith must be in the proper person or it is *not* saving faith. Peter said, "Neither is there salvation in any other: for there is none other name under heaven given among men, whereby we must be saved" (Acts 4:12). You can be sincere and sincerely wrong, and Isaiah warns God's people that faith in Egypt is sinful faith. Egypt is a type of this world and faith in this world's resources instead of God's grace is still sinful.

I. Their ADVICE Was Sinful.
   "that take counsel, but not of me."
   A. Their *counsel* was not of God.
   B. Their *covering* was not of the Spirit.
   C. Their *confidence* was not in Heaven.

II. Their ARSENAL Was Sinful. 30:2, 3
   A. They depended on *a fading Pharoah.*
   B. They depended on *a fleeting shadow.*
   C. They forsook *a faithful God.*

III. Their AMBASSADORS Were Sinful. 30:4-7
   A. They negotiated away their *religion.*
   B. They negotiated away their *riches.*
   C. They negotiated away their *respect.*

Certainly this evil alliance with Egypt was a tragic development in the life of God's people. Sennacherib could be defeated without Egypt's help, and this was proven when the children of Israel listened to Isaiah and heeded his plea to trust wholly in the Lord. Chapters 36 and 37 of Isaiah record for us the destruction of the Assyrian host, *without* the aid of Egypt. Will you not heed this warning and obey?

32.   GOD DOES NOT EAT HIS WORDS
Isaiah 31:2

God is truth. He is not like a man who can lie. God is faithful to His Word. In the verse before us, we read that "God will not call back his words." In other words, God will not eat His words. Many people are hoping He will. Many people are gambling that He will. But He will not! Paul warns us: "Be not deceived; God is not mocked: for whatsoever a man soweth, that shall he also reap" (Galatians 6:7). With reference to God's Word, the Lord Jesus Christ said, "Till heaven and earth pass, one jot or one title shall in no wise pass from the law, till all be fulfilled" (Matthew 5:18).

I. His Word Concerning FLESH Will Stand. 31:1-3
   A. Flesh is characterized by *infidelity to Scripture.*
   B. Flesh is characterized by *inferiority to the Spirit.*
   C. Flesh is characterized by *insubordination to Sovereignty.*
   D. This Word is summarized in Romans 8:5-8

II. His Word Concerning FAITHFULNESS Will Stand. 31:4-6
   A. God will *defend* His people.
   B. God will *deliver* His people.
   C. God will *debase* His enemies.

III. His Word Concerning the FUTURE Will Stand.
   A. God *predicts* the *destiny* of nations.
   B. God *plots* the *destruction* of idolatry.
   C. God *plans* the *direction* of His people.

The Word of God stands! God will not eat His words. He will not call back His words. His Word is forever settled in Heaven, and wise is the man who heeds its warnings and takes hold of its promises.

33. THE MIGHTY GOD-MAN
Isaiah 32:2

Paul wrote: "And without controversy great is the mystery of godliness: God was manifest in the flesh" (I Timothy 3:16). God was manifest in the flesh! What a mighty God and what a mighty man! The Lord Jesus Christ was always master of every situation in which He found Himself here on earth. He always had the right answer. He always had sufficient resources. He always provided what was needed. Isaiah describes the Messiah in the second verse of Chapter 32, and this description shows us again how marvelous is our Saviour.

I. A Great STABILITY.

"an hiding place from the wind."
   A. Stability against the *deceptions* of men. Ephesians 4:14
   B. Stability against the *doctrines* of devils. I Timothy 4:1
   C. Stability against the *discouragements* of indifference.

II. A Great SHELTER.

"a covert from the tempest."
   A. Shelter from the tempest of *turmoil*. John 16:33
   B. Shelter from the tempest of *trial*. II Corinthians 12:9
   C. Shelter from the tempest of *tragedy*. Romans 8:28

III. A Great SOURCE.

"rivers of water in a dry place."
   A. A *pure* source. Hebrews 7:26
   B. A *productive* source. John 4:14
   C. A *plentiful* source, "rivers."

IV. A Great SHADOW.

"the shadow of a great rock."
   A. Shadow from the *heat* of persecution.
   B. Shadow from the *heartaches* of life.
   C. Shadow from the *headaches* of labor.

Jesus said, "Come unto me, all ye that labor and are heavy laden, and I will give you rest. Take my yoke upon you, and learn of me; for I am meek and lowly in heart: and ye shall find rest unto your souls" (Matthew 11:28, 29).

34. THINE EYES SHALL SEE THE KING
Isaiah 33:17

The believer is "looking for that blessed hope, and the glorious appearing of the great God and our Saviour Jesus Christ" (Titus 2:13). And Isaiah tells us, "Thine eyes shall see the king in his beauty." What beauty He possesses! What bliss it will be to gaze upon that One who loved us and gave Himself for us! When we think of the beauty of our King, at least three lines of thought come to our attention. Let us consider them in this message, as we think upon the King "in his beauty."

I. Beautiful in His ATTRIBUTES.
- A. A flawless character.
- B. A faultless conduct.
- C. A faithful Christ.

II. Beautiful in His ACCOMPLISHMENTS.
- A. As God's *Son* — God's *gift.* Romans 6:23
- B. As Heaven's *Sovereign* — God's *governor.* Isaiah 9:7
- C. As Man's *Saviour* — God's *grace.* Ephesians 2:8, 9

III. Beautiful in His ASPIRATIONS.
- A. He is the Planner of our ways.
- B. He is the Protector of our welfare.
- C. He is the Provider of our wealth.

Paul writes: "For our conversation is in heaven; from whence also we look for the Saviour, the Lord Jesus Christ: Who shall change our vile body, that it may be fashioned like unto his glorious body" (Philippians 3:20, 21). Praise God, we shall not only see Him, but we shall be like Him!

35. THE BATTLE OF ARMAGEDDON
Isaiah 34

The Valley of Jezreel and the Plain of Esdraelon at the foot of Mount Megiddo were the scene of many decisive battles and events in the history of Israel. Here occurred the victory sung by Deborah and Barak (Judges 5); Gideon's defeat of Midian (Judges 6); Saul's death at the hands of the Philistines (I Samuel 31 and II Samuel 4); Josiah slain by Pharoah-Nechoh (II Kings 23); and the death of King Ahaziah (II Kings 9). But the greatest and most decisive battle is yet to be fought there. This is the battle which has come to be known as "The Battle of Armageddon." Listen to Isaiah's predictive account of what will take place in that great day of the Lord.

I. The ACCLAMATION of the Prophet. Isaiah 34:1-4
   A. The battle has *international meaning,* "ye nations."
   B. Victory is thru *infallible might.* 34:2, 3
   C. It is an *irrevocable mission.* 34:4

II. The ANGER of the Holy God. Isaiah 34:5, 6
   A. *Justice* must be carried out.
   B. *Judgment* must be consummated.
   C. *Jehovah* must conquer.

III. The ALTERNATIVE to the Sovereignty of Christ. Isaiah 34:7
   A. *Fearful consequences reaped.* When Israel rejected Christ, they said to Pilate: "His blood be on us, and on our children" (Matthew 27:25). What fearful things have come upon a Christ-rejecting world! Isaiah says, "Their land shall be soaked with blood" (Isaiah 34:7).
   B. *Final condemnation reaped.* 34:8

Your personal relationship to God has eternal consequences. Do you know Christ as your personal Saviour and Sovereign? Or are you heading for terrible judgment? Accept Christ now!

36. THE MIRACLE OF CONVERSION
Isaiah 35:1-10

The world-wide millennial reign of Christ will be a miracle of God. We believe Christ will reign literally on the throne of David. In a very real sense, however, there can be millennial joy in the heart of every believer now in this life. What will be true physically in the millennium can be true spiritually now in the heart and life of every believer in Christ. Thus we shall apply this thirty-fifth chapter to the believer today.

I. The Desert Shall Blossom As a Rose. Isaiah 35:1, 2
   A. We should be *fruit-bearing*. Galatians 5:22, 23
   B. We should be *singing*. Psalm 40:1-3
   C. We should be *glorying*. II Corinthians 3:18

II. The Eyes of the Blind Shall Be Opened. Isaiah 35:5a
   A. *Taught* by the *Spirit* of truth. I Corinthians 2:9, 10
   B. *Triumphant* in the *Son* of truth. John 8:36
   C. *Trusting* in the *Scripture* of truth. Pslam 119:105

III. The Ears of the Deaf Shall Be Unstopped. Isaiah 35:5b
   A. Open to the *wooing* of the Spirit. Romans 8:15, 16
   B. Open to the *wail* of the unsaved.
   C. Open to the *Word* of God.

IV. The Lame Shall Leap. Isaiah 35:6
   A. *Victory* over temptations.
   B. *Release* from sinful habits.
   C. *Ability* to be an overcomer.

V. The Parched Ground Shall Become a Pool. Isaiah 35:7
   A. A blessing instead of a curse.
   B. A help instead of a hindrance.
   C. A stepping-stone instead of a stumbling-block.

37. THE DEVIL'S DEVICES
Isaiah 36

Rabshakeh is a picture of the Devil. He used the same methods of intimidation and deceit that the Devil has used for millenniums against the children of God. Paul wrote to the Corinthians, "We are not ignorant of his [Satan's] devices" (II Corinthians 2:11). Fortunately for Israel, their leaders, Hezekiah and Isaiah, were not ignorant of the devil's devices. In this passage of Scripture we may learn much about that evil one's devices and methods of operation.

I. He SUGGESTS That Our Faith Is Unfounded. Isaiah 36:6, 7

    A. He *misrepresents* our faith, "thou trusteth on Egypt."
    B. He *maligns* our faith, "is it not he?"
    C. He *masks* his destructive intent.

II. He SLANDERS the God of Our Faith. Isaiah 36:7

    A. His questions are *misleading*.
    B. His claims are *mistaken*.
    C. His challenge is *mockery*.

III. He SEDUCES with Promises of Material Reward for Those Who Yield. Isaiah 36:8, 16

    A. He appeals to the *senses* of man.
    B. He appeals to the *secular* in man.
    C. He appeals to the *security* desired by man.
    D. He cannot really *satisfy* in any of these areas.

IV. He SWEARS He Is of God. Isaiah 36:10

    A. He claims *orders* from God.
    B. He claims *obedience* to God.

"Satan himself is transformed into an angel of light. Therefore it is no great thing if his ministers also be transformed as the ministers of righteousness; whose end shall be according to their works" (II Corinthians 11:13-15).

38. THE DISSOLVING OF A DILEMMA
Isaiah 37

The challenge of Rabshakeh and the Assyrians was a threat to everything which God's people stood for in that day. But Hezekiah knew where to go with his problem — he went to the Lord. With destruction facing his kingdom and captivity a very real probability for his people, Hezekiah stood firmly in the conviction that the God of Abraham, Isaac and Jacob would deliver.

I. The DILEMMA Facing the Faithful. Isaiah 37:3, 4
- A. The *reproach* against the living God by Rabshakeh.
- B. The *reality* of Assyria's mighty hosts.
- C. The *remnant* of Israel and their weakness militarily.

II. The DEPENDENCE of the Faithful upon God. Isaiah 37:14-20
- A. The *problem related.*
- B. The *power reviewed.* 37:18
- C. The *prayer requested.* 37:20a
- D. The *purpose revealed.* 37:20b

III. The DELIVERANCE Accomplished. Isaiah 37:36-38
- A. God's *answer sure.* 37:33 ff.
- B. God's *action swift.*
- C. God's *adversary smitten.* 37:38

Hezekiah's experience should encourage our hearts to be faithful in prayer. We need to believe God's promises and rest in God's power. Deliverance can be accomplished for us. Each dilemma in life has a solution in God's wisdom and power. Let us trust Him for it.

39. IT'S YOUR TURN TO DIE!
Isaiah 38:1

Can you imagine the thoughts which must have raced through Hezekiah's mind when the message of Isaiah was made known to him? He must have looked into Isaiah's eyes with shocked disbelief. But is it not true that Isaiah's message is applicable to each one of us? "Set thine house in order: for thou shalt die, and not live." The writer of Hebrews tells us that "it is appointed unto man once to die." Since this is so, we should heed the message of the great prophet Isaiah.

I. The ADVISABILITY of an Orderly House, "set thine house in order."
    A. Is your house in order *spiritually?*
        1. Do you set a *Scriptural* example?
        2. Do you worship together in a *sound* church?
        3. Are your children *saved?*
    B. Is your house in order *educationally?*
        1. Is the Bible a part of your family life?
        2. Do good Christian books line your book shelves?
        3. Have you made preparation for your children's education?
    C. Is your house in order *financially?*
        1. Have you remembered God in *your will?*
        2. Do you have treasure in Heaven?

II. The INEVITABILITY of Death, "thou shalt die."
    A. The sentence has been passed.
    B. The execution will surely come.

III. The UNCERTAINTY of Life, "and not live."
    A. It is *valuable.* Mark 8:36, 37
    B. But it is a *vapor.* James 4:14
    C. It will *vanish.*

In light of this truth, prepare to meet thy God by accepting God's gift of eternal life through Jesus Christ our Lord.

40.   JUDGMENT DEMANDED
Isaiah 39

The thirty-ninth chapter of Isaiah climaxes the message of coming judgment which Isaiah has proclaimed. This book of prophecy is divided into two sections: the first thirty-nine chapters look toward the coming judgment and captivity of God's people; the last twenty-seven chapters look forward to the restoration and glory beyond the captivity. Chapter 39 declares again the inflexible purpose of God to bring His wrath upon His people. Judgment is demanded because:

I. God's PROPHETS Have Gone UNHEEDED.
   A.   God's *methods* have been *ridiculed.*
   B.   God's *men* have been *rejected.*
   C.   God's *message* has been *refused.*

II. God's PURPOSES Have Gone UNHONORED.
   A.   The nation's *priests* have *perverted* the true religion.
   B.   The nation's *politicians polluted* government.
   C.   The *people prostituted* their heritage.

III. God's PEOPLE Have Gone UNHARNESSED.
   A.   *Idolatry* was *respected.*
   B.   *Iniquity* was *rampant.*
   C.   *Immorality* was *relative.*
   D.   *Intoxication* was *riotous.*

Upon such a nation's degeneracy was called down the judgment of God. Only the retribution of condemnation and captivity could climax such a record of failure and shame. And be sure that we in America can expect nothing better if we continue our mad plunge down the road of immorality and drunkenness and atheistic lawlessness. "Righteousness exalteth a nation, but sin is a reproach to any people."

41. BEHOLD YOUR GOD!
Isaiah 40:9-26

When man is at his worst, God is at His best. God's people were in captivity to sin and soon to be in captivity to Babylon. Isaiah's message and cry was "Behold your God!" Are you bound by sin? Are you a captive to the lust of the flesh, the lust of the eyes, and the pride of life? Then look to God! Look and live! We live in a generation that looks at everything but God. What will you find when you behold your God?

I. You Will Find Him MAGNIFICENT as a SHEPHERD. Isaiah 40:10, 11

    A. His *pastures* are *plentiful,* "He shall feed his flock."
    B. His *paths* are *purposeful,* "shall gently lead."
    C. His *people* are *prolific,* "those that are with young."

II. You Will Find Him MARVELOUS As a SCIENTIST. Isaiah 40:12-17

    A. His *creation* is *measureless.*
    B. His *comprehension* is *matchless.*
    C. His *counsel* is *miraculous.*
    D. His *concerns* are *multitudinous.*

III. You Will Find Him MIGHTY As a SAVIOUR. Isaiah 40:26-31

    A. He *redeems* the *souls* of His people.
    B. He *restores* the *strength* of His people.
    C. He *revives* the *staggering.*
    D. He *renews* the *swooning.*
    E. He *rejoices* the *spirits* of His people.

Do you need guidance? Behold your Shepherd! Do you need wisdom? Behold your Scientist! Do you need salvation? Behold your Saviour! Behold your God!

42. STRIKING COMPARISONS
Isaiah 41

This is a universe of contrast. In a perfect harmony of unity there is yet melodic diversity. There are beauties to behold through the telescope. There are likewise wonders to be seen through the microscope. The thunder has a majestic sound, but it is no more mysterious than what we hear through the stethoscope. The contrast is seen no more boldly than when it is presented by the Prophet Isaiah in this chapter. Notice at least three contrasts pointed out by the Prophet.

I. The CREATOR and the CREATURE.
   - A. God the *Worker* — man the *worm*. 41:4, 14
   - B. God the *Timeless One* — man the *transcient one*. 4:4
   - C. God the *Master* — man the *servant*.

II. The RICH and the POOR. Isaiah 41:17-20
   - A. God the *Nourisher* — man the *needy*.
   - B. God the *Satisfier* — man the *thirsty* one.
   - C. God the *Wealthy* One — man the *weak* one.

III. The FINISHED WORK and the FLIMSY VANITY. Isaiah 41:10, 11, 28, 29
   - A. God's work is *permanent* — man's is *passing*.
   - B. God's work is *valuable* — man's is *vanity*.
   - C. God's work is *constructive* — man's is *destructive*.

God says, "For my thoughts are not your thoughts, neither are your ways my ways. For as the heavens are higher than the earth, so are my ways higher than your ways, and my thoughts than your thoughts" (Isaiah 55:8, 9). What a tremendous contrast!

43. I AM THE LORD: THAT IS MY NAME
Isaiah 42:8-12

The God of the Bible is exclusively unique. He alone is the Lord. He alone deserves our worship and service. In the passage before us, Isaiah quotes the Lord's message of personal testimony. In these verses He tells of His very exclusiveness.

I. His PRAISE Is Exclusive. Isaiah 42:8
   A. He does not *divide* His glory *with* others.
   B. He does not *delegate* His glory *to* others.
   C. He does not *desecrate* His glory *through* idolatry.

II. His PROPHECY Is Exclusive. Isaiah 42:9
   A. *Past success* declares this "the former things."
   B. *Present Scriptures* declare this "new things do I declare."
   C. *Future situations* will confirm this "before they spring forth."

III. His PEOPLE Are Exclusive. Isaiah 42:10-12
   A. They are a *redeemed people*.
   B. They are a *royal priesthood*.
   C. They have a *reserved place*.

"Now therefore ye are no more strangers and foreigners, but fellow citizens with the saints, and of the household of God; and are built upon the foundation of the apostles and prophets, Jesus Christ himself being the chief corner stone" (Ephesians 2:19, 20).

44. THE SUPER SIN BLOTTER
Isaiah 43:25

David prayed out of the distress of his soul: "My sin is ever before me" (Psalm 51:3). Is not this the cry of every convicted sinner? My sin is ever before me! For those in such distress, Isaiah has good news! The message of forgiveness of sin through the death, burial and resurrection of Jesus Christ is indeed the gospel — the good news. Isaiah tells how we may find relief and remission, pardon and peace, cleansing from sin and calmness of soul. Let us read his message with joy.

I. The INDELIBILITY of Man's Sin.
   A. It is deeply *ingrained* in man's heart. Isaiah 1:18
   B. It is deeply *inscribed* in God's books. Revelation 20: 12, 13
   C. It is deeply *imbedded* in man's conscience. Romans 2:14, 15

II. The INFINITY of God's Memory.
   A. He *sees* the heart. I Samuel 16:7
   B. He *searches* the heart. Jeremiah 17:9, 10

III. The INTENTION of God's Offer.
"for my own sake."
   A. God's holiness *vindicated*. Romans 3:1-4
   B. God's mercy *verified*. Titus 3:5
   C. God's love *validated*. John 3:16

IV. The IMMENSITY of God's Grace.
"will not remember your sins."
   A. He remembers the sinner but not the sin. Luke 23:42
   B. He remembers our origin but not our sin. Psalm 103: 12-14
   C. He eradicates our sin from His books eternally.

This is such good news that we ought to be telling it to others every day of every year. This is the gospel with which we are to go into all the world.

45. FRUSTRATION, MADMEN AND FOOLS
Isaiah 44:24-28

The wise of this world have generally downgraded the importance of the Bible. The Word of God has been the object of intellectual scoffings and the subject of satirical penmen many, many times in this so-called enlightened twentieth century. And yet the Bible's message is coming to pass. Things are worsening on the horizons of international and national politics. There are wars and rumors of wars. There is no peace despite much talk about peace. In other words, the very things the Bible prophecies tell of, the very conditions described in the Bible are coming to pass in the world in which we live. Thus it is that Isaiah pictures unbelieving infidels as frustrated liars, mad diviners and foolish wise men. The facts of Isaiah 44:26 guarantee the truth of Isaiah 44:25.

I. FRUSTRATED LIARS.
   A. The *fulfillment* of Scripture frustrates the infidels.
   B. The *future* of Israel frustrates the infidels.
   C. The *faithfulness* of God frustrates the infidels.

II. FORTUNE-TELLING MADMEN.
   A. Man's *predictions* have *failed.*
   B. Man's *predicaments* have *flourished.*
   C. Man's *purposes* have *failed.*
   D. Man's *pavilions* have *fallen.*

III. FOOLISH KNOWLEDGE.
   A. Reprobate minds.
   B. Rebellious wills.
   C. Rejecting hearts.

The Word of our God shall stand forever! It is an anvil upon which the agnostics of centuries have broken their hammers of unbelief. But the anvil remains.

46. MAN VERSUS GOD
Isaiah 45:9-24

"Woe unto him who fights with his Maker," declares the Prophet Isaiah. Man has not even an outside chance of winning the battle, but he fights foolishly on, "because the carnal mind is enmity against God: for it is not subject to the law of God, neither indeed can be" (Romans 8:7). There are reasons why man is hopelessly futile in his opposition to God: hence, Isaiah's "Woe."

I. God As the Creator Is SUPREME. Isaiah 45:12
   - A. *Humanity* is His *creation*.
   - B. The *Heavens* are His *concern*.
   - C. The *hosts* of Heaven are at His *command*.

II. God As the Author Is SUFFICIENT. Isaiah 45:19
   - A. God's Word has been *revealed*, "I have not spoken in secret."
   - B. God's willingness is *real*, "I said not . . . seek ye me in vain."
   - C. God's Word is *righteous*, "I declare things that are right."
   - D. God's Word is *replete*.

III. God As the King Is SOVEREIGN. Isaiah 45:22-25
   - A. *Salvation* for believers. 45:22
   - B. *Shame* for unbelievers. 45:24b
   - C. *Satisfaction* for Israel. 45:25

Why not be reconciled to God now? Stop your foolish and useless opposition to the will and Word of God and trust Christ as your Saviour and Lord today.

47. SANCTIFIED MEMORY
Isaiah 46:8, 9

It is good to recall often that "once I was blind, but now I can see." The Prophet exhorts the people to "remember." By this he does not mean a morbid concentration on the sins of the past. He does not refer to an unhealthy preoccupation with the failures of the past. But he does encourage the people to take heart from the past. He does exhort them to learn from the past. He does ask them to be humbled by remembering what God has saved them from in the past. "Remember!"

I. Remember the FUTILITY of Idolatry. Isaiah 46:7, 8
   - A.   The *sensual* idolatry of pleasure. II Timothy 3:4
   - B.   The *aesthetic* idolatry of religion. II Timothy 3:5
   - C.   The *intellectual* idolatry of science. II Timothy 3:7
   - D.   Remember the *inability* of these to save. Isaiah 46:7

II. Remember the FORMER things. Isaiah 46:9; Deuteronomy 32:7-30
   - A.   God *chose* Israel among the nations.
   - B.   God *cared* for them in the wilderness.
   - C.   God *cursed* their enemies.
   - D.   God *chided* Israel for their unfaithfulness

III. Remember the FAITHFULNESS of God. Isaiah 46:10, 11
   - A.   It is His *prophecy* that is faithfully fulfilled.
   - B.   It is His *pleasure* that is faithfully executed.
   - C.   It is His *purpose* that is faithfully carried out.

"But the mercy of the Lord is from everlasting to everlasting upon them that fear him, and his righteousness unto children's children; to such as keep his covenant, and to those that REMEMBER his commandments to do them" (Psalm 103:17, 18).

48. COME, SIT AND HEAR!
Isaiah 47

In this chapter Isaiah gives some short orders. The commands are terse and to the point but full of meaning. In this generation of "hustle and bustle," "hurry and worry," we need to heed these commands. Let us examine them.

I. Come Down — HUMBLING. Isaiah 47:1
  A. Down from the *pedestal* of pride.
  B. Down from the *podium* of self-righteousness. Isaiah 64:6
  C. Down from the *platform* of self-sufficiency. Luke 18:17
  D. Down to the *position* of a sinner.

II. Sit Thou Silent — HALLOWING. Isaiah 47:5
  A. Stop *conversing* with the world.
  B. Start *contemplating* God. Psalm 46:10
  C. Settle *conviction* in His presence.

III. Hear now — HEARKENING. Isaiah 47:8-10; Hebrews 3:7, 8
  A. Self-confidence is dangerous.
  B. Slack-carelessness is dooming.
  C. Sinful complacency is degrading.

IV. Stand now — HONESTY. Isaiah 47:12-15
  A. Admit you have *failed.*
  B. Confess your *faithlessness.*
  C. Own up to the *futility* of your gods.
  D. Confess your need.

We will add one final request — Accept Christ now!

49. WHY NO PEACE?
Isaiah 48:22

"There is no peace, saith the Lord, unto the wicked." Why is this so? Why is it that the unregenerate, unsaved individual has no real peace of mind and heart? There are at least three reasons.

I. The Sinner Has a REPROVING CONSCIENCE. Romans 2:14, 15
  - A. It is *restless* amid the *activity* of sin.
  - B. It is *relentless* in its *accusation* of the sinner.
  - C. It is *rebellious* in its *accommodation* to the sinner.

II. The Sinner Harbors a REBELLIOUS CARNALITY. Romans 8:5-8
  - A. It gives no peace because it does not satisfy even the flesh.
  - B. It gives no peace because it does not satisfy the spirit.
  - C. It gives no peace because it does not satisfy the mind.
  - D. The quest for carnal satisfaction only adds confusion.

III. The Sinner Heads for a RECKONING CONCLUSION. Revelation 20:12-15
  - A. Death is an *unwanted misery*.
  - B. Eternity is an *unknown mystery*.
  - C. The judgment is an *undesired meeting*.
  - D. The Lake of Fire has *undreamed* of *meaning*.

No wonder there is no peace for the wicked. They are not, they admit, sure where they came from. They are not sure why they are here. And they are uncertain as to the future. How perfect would be their peace if they would trust Christ, who is "the way, the truth, and the life."

50. JUDGMENT AND REWARD
Isaiah 49:4

"Surely my judgment is with the Lord, and my work with my God," writes Isaiah. Judgment is a vital theme in the Bible. Final judgment is coming for every man. It is very important to note that the final judgments do *not* have anything to do with eternal destiny. Your eternal destiny is decided *before* you leave this earth. That destiny is decided on the basis of what you do with the Lord Jesus Christ. The Bible says, "He that believeth on the Son hath everlasting life: and he that believeth not the Son shall not see life; but the wrath of God abideth on him" (John 3:36). Therefore, the Judgment Seat of Christ is only for believers, those who have accepted Christ and are eternally saved. The Great White Throne Judgment is for sinners who are already eternally doomed. These judgments have to do with rewards for believers and degrees of punishment for unbelievers. The question of eternal destiny is not at stake at the final judgments. That question has already been settled by that time. In thinking of judgment, three things are certain.

I. Judgment Will Be according to OPPORTUNITY.
   A. *Illustrated* by Parable of Talents. Matthew 25:14-30
   B. *Instruction* by Paul. I Corinthians 12:18-20

II. Judgment Will Be according to OBEDIENCE. II John 8

III. Judgment Will Be according to OMNISCIENCE. Colossians 3:21-25
   A. He *respects* no person.
   B. He *rewards* every person.

51. THE POWER OF GOD
Isaiah 50:2, 3

The two verses before us are a commentary on the power of God. The statement on the power of God recorded in verses 2 and 3, comes after six questions asked in verses 1 and 2. Our generation is the most power conscious in history. We are obsessed with power. We are so preoccupied with our power that we tend to forget omnipotence. We tend to forget that God is all-powerful and almighty. Our power when compared to His is as a drop of water to an ocean.

I. God Has Power over Man's HABITAT. Job 38
  A. The waters are under His *control.*
  B. The creatures are at His *command.*
  C. The heavens are under His *commission.*

II. God Has Power over Man's HAUGHTINESS. Luke 1: 52, 53
  A. He puts down the *haughty.*
  B. He raises up the *humble.*
  C. He feeds the *hungry.*
  D. He deprives the *healthy.*
  E. He reveals the *hypocrite.*

III. God Has Power over Man's HABITS. II Corinthians 5:17; I Thessalonians 5:23, 24
  A. He delivered a blasphemer like Paul.
  B. He set at liberty a libertine like Augustine.
  C. He freed a drunkard like Mel Trotter.

"I am not ashamed of the gospel of Christ, for it is the POWER of God unto salvation to everyone that believeth: to the Jew first and also to the Greek" (Romans 1:16).

52. INVENTORY-TAKING TIME
Isaiah 51

Chapter 51 of Isaiah is inventory time for "ye that follow after righteousness, ye that seek the Lord." Most people take some kind of inventory around New Year's Day, but really we ought to do it more often. We need carefully and honestly to evaluate our strong points and our weak points and then, by God's grace set out to profit from the evaluation.

I. A GLIMPSE at the Past. Isaiah 51:1, 2
   - A. A *rock* of help.
   - B. A *reason* for hope.
   - C. A *relationship* of blessing.

II. A GRACE for the Present. Isaiah 51:3-10
   - A. *Comfort* is promised. 51:3, 4
   - B. *Change* is forecast. 51:5, 6
   - C. *Courage* is recommended. 51:7, 8
   - D. *Clothing* is prescribed. 51:9, 10

III. A GUARANTEE for the Future. Isaiah 51:11-16
   - A. A return of rejoicing for the redeemed. 51:11
   - B. A God of comfort for the captives. 51:12, 13
   - C. A God of omnipotence for the oppressed. 51:14-16

IV. A GATHERING to God. Isaiah 51:17-23
   - A. Fury *finished*.
   - B. Faith *fulfilled*.
   - C. Future *fortressed*.

This was a message of hope that enabled the captives to endure the hardness and the heartache. Certainly our blessed hope ought to encourage us to "endure hardness as good soldiers of Jesus Christ."

53.   BEAUTIFUL FOOTWORK
Isaiah 52:7

Part of being properly equipped for the good fight of faith is having "your feet shod with the preparation of the gospel of peace" (Ephesians 6:15). Isaiah says that such feet are "beautiful." How desperately in need the world is today of "beautiful feet." In Romans 10:14 and 15, Paul asks: "How shall they hear without a preacher? and how shall they preach except they be sent? . . . How beautiful are the feet of them. . . ." How we need to be missionaries with the Good News of the gospel!

I. The PLACE of the Feet, "upon the mountains."
    A. The gospel must not be *hidden.*
    B. The gospel must be *heralded.*
    C. The gospel must be *hastened.*

II. The PEACE of the Feet.
    A. *Good tidings* — sins forgiven.
    B. *Great triumph* — God is faithful.
    C. *Genuine tranquility* — grace's fortune.

III. The PUBLISHING of the Feet.
    A. A proclamation of *salvation.*
    B. A broadcast of *sovereignty,* "Thy God reigneth."
    C. A concert of *singing.* 52:8

Jesus said, "Follow me, and I will make you fishers of men" (Matthew 4:19). If you are walking in paths of righteousness for His name's sake, then you should be one of whom it can be said, "What beautiful feet!"

54. THE SUPERB SUBSTITUTE
Isaiah 53:1-6

Chapter 53 of Isaiah is one of the best-known and best-loved passages in the Bible. The message of the gospel is so movingly given in this chapter. Christ is presented as our Substitute, the One who took our place. Perhaps Peter had this passage in mind when he wrote, "For Christ also hath once suffered for sins, the just for the unjust, that he might bring us to God" (I Peter 3:18). This is the blessed message of this chapter.

I. Christ's Life Was SINLESS.
   A. The righteous leaders could find no sin in Him.
   B. The Roman law could find no fault with Him.
   C. He was the spotless Lamb of God. Hebrews 7:26

II. Christ's Death Was SACRIFICIAL.
   A. It was a *voluntary* death. John 10:11, 18
   B. It was a *valuable* death. I Peter 1:18
   C. It was a *victorious* death. John 19:30

III. Christ's Atonement Was SUBSTITUTIONARY. Isaiah 53:4-6
   A. He was wounded for our wrongs.
   B. He was tried for our transgressions.
   C. He was smitten for our sins.
   D. He was slain for our salvation.

Truly He was the superb and supreme substitute. He did what no other could do and what no other would do. He is God's provision for you. Right now will you accept it by accepting Him?

55. THE NECESSITY OF EXPANSION
Isaiah 54:2

The interpretation of our text is with reference to the nation Israel. However, we want to apply the words of Isaiah to our responsibilities as believers. The challenge is, "Enlarge the place of thy tent." If we are to reach the multitudes with the gospel, we must enlarge our vision, we must expand our efforts, we must launch out into new areas with our message. Numbers are important, for numbers do represent individuals with precious and eternal souls. We must enlarge our place because:

I. The POPULATION DEMANDS It.
   A. A population explosion demands a missionary expansion.
   B. A spiritually blind population needs the Great Physician.
   C. A hell-bound population needs the Saviour.

II. The PREACHER DEPENDS on It.
   A. Expanded *facilities* are needed.
   B. Enlarged *finances* are needed.
   C. Enlightened *faith* is needed.

III. The PROVISION DESERVES It.
   A. "God so loved the world."
   B. Christ is the propitiation "for the sins of the whole world."
   C. We are commissioned to go to "all nations" (Matthew 28:19).
   D. We are commanded to "preach the gospel to every creature."

Our day calls for an enlarging of the place of our tent. The world must hear, and they will not hear if we fail to give top priority to this great task of proclaiming the gospel.

56. ABUNDANT PARDON
Isaiah 55

Salvation is not probation; it is pardon. God offers us complete deliverance from the guilt and penalty of sin through His Son, the Lord Jesus Christ. Isaiah speaks in this chapter of this abundant pardon which God gives.

I. His Pardon Is AVAILABLE. Isaiah 55:1, 2
  A. It is the *gift* of God.
  B. It is the *gratification* of our need.

II. His Pardon Is ACCESSIBLE. Isaiah 55:6
  A. He may be found today.
  B. He may be called upon today.
  C. Tomorrow may very well be too late. Proverbs 27:1

III. His Pardon Is ABUNDANT. Isaiah 55:7
  A. Forsake your wicked *iniquity*.
  B. Forsake your *imaginations*.
  C. Accept God's *invitation*.

IV. His Pardon Is AMAZING. Isaiah 55:8, 9
  A. Conceived in infinite wisdom.
  B. Carried out in infinite ways.

V. His Pardon Is ABOUNDING. Isaiah 55:10, 11
  A. The Word of Pardon is *preached*.
  B. The Word of Pardon is *planted*.
  C. The Word of Pardon is *prosperous*.

VI. His Pardon Is ADORNING. Isaiah 55:12, 13
  A. Joy is its *thrill*.
  B. Peace is its *theme*.
  C. Strength is its *testimony*.

Will you accept your pardon today? A pardon is not effective unless it is accepted, and you must do the accepting.

57. MAJORING ON THE MAJORS
Isaiah 56:4-5

"For thus saith the Lord unto the eunuchs that keep my sabbaths, and choose the things that please me, and take hold of my covenant; Even unto them will I give in mine house and within my walls a place and a name better than of sons and daughters." God is pleased with these men who "choose the things" that please Him. Many today are sacrificing permanent values on the altar of immediate expediency. Many are majoring on the minors and minoring on the majors. What are some of the values we need to get straight?

I. TIME Is Secondary to ETERNITY. Luke 12:16-21
   A. The "here" only takes on real meaning when rightly related to the "hereafter."
   B. Living for this old world only is being time-wise and eternity-foolish.

II. EARTHLY Is Secondary to HEAVENLY.
   A. Our affections should be in heaven. Colossians 3:2
   B. Our citizenship should be in heaven. Philippians 3:20

III. PHYSICAL Is Secondary to SPIRITUAL.
   A. *Spiritual fitness* should be our real concern. I Timothy 4:8
   B. *Sinful folly* is but for a season. Hebrews 11:24-26

IV. RELIGION Is Secondary to SALVATION.
   A. Christianity more important than Churchianity.
   B. Faith more important than formalism.
   C. Christ more important than ceremonies.
   D. Righteousness more important than rites.

Let's put first things first. Let's "choose the things that please God." Jesus said, "I do always those things that please him" (John 8:29). Let us follow His example.

58. THE SIN OF ADULTERY
Isaiah 57

Adultery is one of the prevalent sins of America. But the sin of religious adultery is even more prevalent. We have been unfaithful to our God officially, educationally, economically, nationally and religiously. But in this message we want to discuss the sin of adultery toward God as individuals. Are you faithless? Then listen to Isaiah's message.

I. The SPIRIT of Adultery. Isaiah 57:7-10
   A. Pride in *self*. 57:7
   B. A false *secretiveness* and false security. 57:8
   C. A perfumed and covered-up *stench*. 57:9
   D. A damnable determination. 57:10; Proverbs 6:32

II. The SHAME of Adultery. Isaiah 57:11-14
   A. No *remembrance* of God. 57:11
   B. No *remuneration*. 57:12
   C. No *relief* in that which you trusted. 57:13

III. The SAVIOUR from Adultery. Isaiah 57:15, 16
   A. A Holy Saviour's conditions. 57:15
   B. A humble sinner's contrition.

What a great sin adultery is! How quickly God will forgive if we but turn to Him in true repentance and faith. He will cleanse and give victory. Will you trust Him?

59. FASTING OR FAMINE — WHICH?
Isaiah 58:1-11

It is popular in most American communities today to be respectably religious. It was also thus in Israel even when the people had not one iota of spiritual understanding. In this chapter, Isaiah records God's displeasure with the people for their emphasis on vain religion instead of on virtuous right. The people boasted of their fasting but in reality were in the midst of a spiritual famine.

I. Sinners Use RELIGIOUS WORKS As a CLOCK.
   A. This reveals an *ignorance* of the sinfulness of sin. 58:1, 2
   B. This reveals an *incapacity* to understand God. 58:3
   C. This reveals a selfish *interest* in social position. 58:4; Matthew 6:16-18
   D. Such religious works reveal a famine of godliness and mock true fasting.

II. God Requires REPENTANT WILLS As a CONDITION for Blessing. Isaiah 58:5-7
   A. This involves a *renouncing* of sin.
   B. This involves *restoration*.
   C. This involves *relieving* the oppressed.

III. REFRESHING WORKS As a CONSEQUENCE. Isaiah 58:8-11
   A. This means *peace*. 58:8
   B. This means *prayer*. 58:9
   C. This means *proclamation*. 58:10, 11

The reliance upon religious works always blights the individual's spiritual progress. Only as the sinner confesses himself to be unworthy and unmeriting is he in a position to call upon God and His grace. The testimony must be that of Titus 3:5 — "Not by works of righteousness which we have done, but according to his mercy he saved us, by the washing of regeneration, and renewing of the Holy Ghost."

60. GOD'S ANSWER TO MAN'S PROBLEM
Isaiah 59:1-21

Three things are noted in these verses which are beyond doubt. First, God's sufficiency. Second, God's willingness to save man. Third, man's sinfulness. Isaiah discusses these three matters in this chapter and thus offers God's answer to man's problem.

I. The PROBLEM, Man's Sin.
- A. The *result* of man's sin. 59:2
- B. The *record* of man's sin. 59:3-9
- C. The *recklessness* of man's sin. 59:10-13

II. The PROVISION, God's Sufficient Power. Isaiah 59:1
- A. His hand is not shortened.
- B. His ear is not heavy.
- C. His eyes are not blinded. 59:15

III. The PROVOCATION, God's Willingness. Isaiah 59:16-21
- A. He loved us first. I John 4:19
- B. He sought us first. Acts 9:5
- C. His Spirit keeps us faithfully.

The answer to man's problem is not in himself. Man's problem can only be answered in God. Man does not even recognize his need often times; so God must take the initiative in seeking and saving the lost. How good it is to know that along with His willingness is His almighty sufficiency!

61. POLITICAL PROSPERITY
Isaiah 60:1-18

The international situation seems to be one of constant turmoil. The Prince of Peace has been rejected and men struggle to solve their mounting problems. The Word of God reveals that a day is coming when Jesus Christ will rule this world in perfect justice and harmony. Isaiah 60 speaks of this time of political prosperity and peace which Christ only can bring about.

I. Only Christ Can Give LIGHT. Isaiah 60:1, 3
- A. *Political* understanding.
- B. *Personal* enlightenment.
- C. *Practical* administration.
- D. All of this is true for the individual today.

II. Only Christ Can Give GLORY. Isaiah 60:2
- A. Man is *humbled*.
- B. God is *hallowed*.
- C. Christ is *honored*.

III. Only Christ Can Give PEACE. Isaiah 60:18
- A. Sin is *destructive*.
- B. Salvation is *constructive*.

IV. Only Christ Can Give PLENTY. Isaiah 60:4-17
- A. Spiritual plenty *first*.
- B. Physical plenty *second*.
- C. *Complete* satisfaction.

Let us say with the Psalmist, "Be wise now therefore, O ye kings: be instructed, ye judges of the earth. Serve the Lord with fear, and rejoice with trembling. Kiss the Son, lest he be angry, and ye perish from the way, when his wrath is kindled but a little. Blessed are all they that put their trust in him" (Psalm 2:10-12).

62.   BEAUTY FOR ASHES
Isaiah 61:3

Sin has glamor but not gracefulness. Sin has blare but not real beauty. Sin has enjoyment but not real joy. Sin has brightly decorated shadows but not real substance. In Isaiah 61:3 God tells us that He is able to give us reality in place of vanity.

I. The Beauty of SALVATION.
   "Beauty for ashes."
   A. Sin's works are *ashes*.
   B. The Saviour's work is *accomplished*.
   C. Salvation is *adornment* for the believer.

II. The Joy of the SPIRIT.
   "The oil of joy for mourning."
   A. Sin's works produce *sorrow*.
   B. Salvation's work provides the *Spirit*.
   C. The Holy Spirit implants the *song* of joy.

III. The Garment of the SAINT.
   A. The sinner's *clothing* is heaviness and *rags*.
   B. The saint's *covering* is praise and *rejoicing*.
   C. Salvation's *commendation* is the robe of *righteousness*.

It takes miraculous power to transform a life in this way. This power is certainly available through Christ who changed water to wine, who fed 5,000 people with a boy's lunch, who raised the dead and made the blind see. Give him your ashes, your mourning, and your heaviness; and he will give you in exchange beauty, joy and praise.

63. WHY THE ARABS CAN'T WIN AND THE JEWS CAN'T LOSE
Isaiah 62:1-12

The land of Palestine has been for centuries a disputed piece of real estate. However, according to God's Word the Arabs are doomed to failure while Israel is destined for victory. God's promise to Abraham has never been abrogated, and Isaiah confirms the fact that God will give Israel the land of promise. We submit three reasons as to why this must come to pass.

    I. The GLORY of God Is Magnified in His Saving of the Weak. Isaiah 62:1-3; Deuteronomy 9:1-6
- A. An *undeserving* people.
- B. An *unknown* people.
- C. An *untaught* people.

   II. The DELIGHT of the Lord Is to Save Israel. Isaiah 62:4, 5
- A. God's *pledge*. Genesis 12:3
- B. Israel's *peculiarity*.
- C. The world's *perplexity*.

  III. The POWER of God Is Sworn to Save Israel. Isaiah 62:6-12
- A. Literally.
- B. Spiritually.
- C. Perpetually.

Current events seem to point to the fact that it will not be long until Isaiah's prophecy comes to complete fulfillment. In the meantime, let us look for that blessed hope and glorious appearing of our great God and Saviour Jesus Christ.

64. WHAT IS THE WORLD COMING TO?
Isaiah 63

Have you ever heard anyone say, "What is the world coming to anyway?" In Isaiah 63, the prophet tells us what the world is coming to. It is coming to a showdown with God Himself.

I. Coming to a Showdown with the POWER of God. Isaiah 63:1
   A. Involving "glorious apparel" — *transfiguration.*
   B. Involving "traveling" — *transportation.*
   C. Involving power to "save" — *transformation.*

II. Coming to a Showdown with the JUDGMENT of God. Isaiah 63:2-6
   A. Involving the *wages* of sin — death. 63:2-4
   B. Involving the *wrath* of God. 63:5, 6
   C. Involving the *weakness* of men, "bring down their strength."

III. Coming to a Showdown with the PURPOSE of God. Isaiah 63:7-19
   A. The *restoration* of Israel.
   B. The *Rulership* of the Lord Jesus Christ.
   C. The *redemption* of believers.

Are you personally ready for a showdown with God? You must meet Him someday, and you are accountable to Him. You cannot escape His power, you cannot appeal His judgment, and you cannot thwart His purposes. Trust Christ as your Saviour and make your meeting with Him a glad day instead of a sad showdown.

65. FROM RAGS TO RICHES
Isaiah 64:6

Years ago Horatio Alger made a name for himself with his popular stories capitalizing on the theme "From Rags to Riches." Isaiah tells us that man in his sinful condition may be described as wearing rags. It is only when the sinner comes to the Saviour that he can properly be described as having come from rags to riches.

   I. The IMPURITY of the Covering.
- A. Our nature is *sinful,* "an unclean thing."
- B. Our ways are *shameful,* "filthy."
- C. Our best is *spurious.*

  II. The INADEQUACY of the Covering.
- A. Rags are *unsuitable.*
- B. Rags are *unsightly.*
- C. Rags of self-righteousness are *unspiritual.*

 III. The IMPERMANENCE of the Covering, "fade."
- A. They are *temporary* as leaves.
- B. They are *taken* away as leaves.
- C. They are *typical* of vanity.

 IV. The ILLUSTRATION of the Covering of Christ.
- A. It is clean.
- B. It is complete.
- C. It is continuing.
- D. It is constant.

What is the story of your life thus far? Are you still living in the poverty of sin? Why not come into the plenty of God's grace? This can be so as you trade your rags of self-righteousness for the rich robes of Christ's righteousness.

66. THE DICTATORSHIP OF DEITY
Isaiah 65:18-25

Recently I read a "sermon topic survey" which revealed that people want to hear very little preaching on death, judgment, hell, and heaven. But Christ is coming, not only to judge but also to rule as a King. He will be the world's first perfect benevolent dictator. In this kingdom we shall see:

I. LAMENTATION REMOVED. Isaiah 65:18, 19
A. *Rejoicing* will be continual.
B. *Remorse* will be forgotten.

II. LONGEVITY RESTORED. Isaiah 65:20
A. Life will be *active*.
B. Life will be *abiding*.

III. LABOR REWARDED. Isaiah 65:21-23
A. Building will be blessed.
B. Planting will be prospered.
C. Savings will be safe.

IV. LAW REINFORCED. Isaiah 65:22, 23
A. *Stealing* of *possessions* will not be permitted.
B. *Seizing* of *property* will not be tolerated.

V. LEADERSHIP REVERED. Isaiah 65:24, 25
A. There will be expert consultation.
B. There will be effective communication.
C. There will be excellent co-operation.

This kind of a world cannot be brought about by the United Nations. It can only be brought into existence by the King of kings and Lord of lords. He can bring such harmony into your life if you will but make him King of your heart.

67.   A GRAND CONCLUSION
Isaiah 66:18-24

The tremendous theme of millennial blessing reaches its climax in the last chapter of Isaiah's great book. It is truly a grand conclusion in every respect.

I. A Grand Conclusion MENTALLY. Isaiah 66:18, 19
  A. Every *thought* will be turned toward God.
  B. Every *tongue* will speak of His glory.
  C. Every *theme* will honor His grace.

II. A Grand Conclusion EMOTIONALLY. Isaiah 66:20, 21
  A. Guilt will be *resolved.*
  B. God and man will be *reconciled.*
  C. Worship will be *received.*

III. A Grand Conclusion PHYSICALLY.
  A. The creation will be *restored.*
  B. The creature will be *renewed.*
  C. The physical will be *redeemed.*

IV. A Grand Conclusion SPIRITUALLY.
  A. *Worship* will be perfect. 66:23
  B. The *worm* will be perpetual. 66:24

In light of all this, let us heed the exhortation of the Apostle Paul in I Corinthians 15:58 — "Therefore, my beloved brethren, be ye stedfast, unmoveable, always abounding in the work of the Lord, forasmuch as ye know that your labor is not in vain in the Lord."